The Birth of Purple

POEMS AND ART

BERNARD FILIPOW

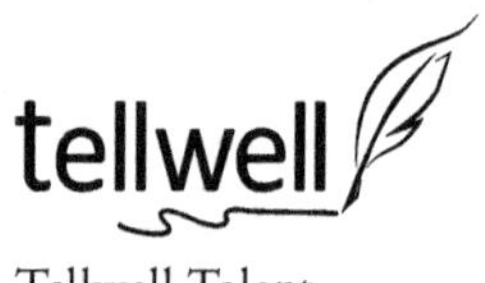

Tellwell Talent
www.tellwell.ca

ISBN
978-0-2288-9004-1 (Hardcover)
978-0-2288-9002-7 (Paperback)
978-0-2288-9003-4 (eBook)

*It is thought by some that the colour purple
evokes creativity and imagination and
resonates strongly with artists of all kinds,
from passionate writers to thoughtful painters.*

ALSO BY BERNARD FILIPOW

Amoresia Love Sonnets 2020
The Blue Tortoise Haiku Poems 2021
Amores Poems 2022

To my children Roseanna, Alexander and
Anthony, and my nephew Christopher.

There she is not -
But only an afterthought.
Her presence historic no more -
Since they finally closed the Captain's door.
Memories of her cheer linger still -
From down below looking up the hill.
Was it the admiral anchor
That somehow sank her?
Theories still persist -
Amidst the legendary "Maid of the Mist".

The kissing trees
With spring-green leaves
Give birth to the breeze
One hears but never sees.

The moon is in cancer,
The lunar clock ticks quarterly,
Aquarius has emptied his vessel,
And Babylonians plant on the morrow.

In gold threaded masks
and robes,
The "chosen people"
paraded on water.
Protected by the gods
and the lions roar
"Le Serenissima", a
miracle a thousand
years old.

Archeologists
Dig with shovel and trowel
Discover with "nose".

No man of letters
Experience was his art
Not words of others.
"Disscepolo Della sperientia".

Confined by covid
Guarded by stands of cedar
And a locked front door!

Birds migrate at night
High to keep their muscles cool
And avoid the wind.

Patience and toughness
Overcame his painful life
As the poet said.

It was not through force
That his life was a success
But through perseverance.

The mighty Niagara drowned
Below its skirring currents
Where it greets the lake and the sky
In the summer's fading light
As music wafted across the waters
And party goers watched from shore
The young crew of the foundered
Foam.

Four million red bricks
Raised skyward to build a dome
"Flower of Firenze".

Which is more noble?
The poet or the painter?
Poem or painting?

Working in a spring garden -
Before all the plants can harden -
Many flowers disappear
Because of errant,
Just-sharpened shears.
'Tis wiser to prune with a spoon
Or wait until the following moon.

Hawks circle rainbows
To beats of primitive drums
And burning sweet grass.

Kite to his cradle
Opened his mouth with its tail
Was it fantasy?

I abandoned friends
Leaning 'gainst meters on Main
Where the time stood still.

Swinging on the oak tree swing
Mesmerized by the green-lighted
spring
Like a bird on the wing in the
upswing.
My heart so light I start to sing.
Such a blissful, unprofane thing
Like pending a knee and praying.

"True love" travels like the wind
Never seen and without passport
Given only those so destined
An enigma constant in a sacred
heart.

     He peeled back layers
     Of both muscle and tissue
     To a mystery.

     In juxtaposing
     The beautiful and ugly
     He became obsessed.

Model of the world
Fitting in circle and square
In earth and heaven.

Hard boiled in egg whites
A receptive organ that sees
By reflected light.

The humdrum diminishes the why
Until I look up into the moonlit sky
Then the question becomes surreal
And I feel the urge to kneel.

The day's sun kissed face
Smiles on me along the way
Adore *Helios*.

Shock and disbelief
Converging on one's forehead
Foretells betrayal.

The young poet's verses lay dormant
Like the seeds of desert flora
'Neath the sand and the blazing sun.
'Twas tragedy that rejuvenated the poet,
Torrential rain the quiescent seeds.
And a poem captured the splendour
Of nature's ways so tender.

      At the piano
      Pencil from mouth to soundboard
      Inspired by moonlight
      And a broken heart.

      I found an empty robin's nest
      And filled it with damp clay
      When I pulled the nest away
      It seemed perfect in nature's
      very own way!
      Of this phenomenon,
      "What would Euclid say?"

The fauvist fairies dancing
with delight
Feather their spring hues
well into the night.
A palette of color now
awakens my sight -
The object of its sense
arrived with the morning
light.

Tell me If you can -
"Is there a halo more brilliant
Than that which enshrouds
A simple, honest man?"

He practiced for years
But on his best performance
He was all alone.

Ten digits forming an unforgettable number
Enrolled us as a party-line member.
Throughout the years, whether punching keys or
dialling
While crying or smiling
Or whether it was long-distance or locally,
It formed part of our rural identity.
An address of a personal kind,
Even when eavesdropping on the line,
And one in my heart's memory forever
enshrined.

Am I going back to before I started?
Makes me wonder why I departed!
And how?
And from where?
No one seems to know.
Is it the final act in this mystery show?

If life's challenges are to
be resolved,
If life's problems are to
be solved
And if life's conflicts are
to be dissolved,
"Tis necessary man
continues to evolve.

In the dullness of a long wait,
I close my eyes
And hear my sighs and
I recall the time and the date.
I think of my life quickly passing by
Of time desolate.
And If, when I die,
Will I have reached a perf state
And winked at dame "fickle fate"?
Or, will I be incomplete
And collapse in anguish at her feet?

Sitting on the porch
Listening to the leafy music of the birch.
It can play every tune
Especially in the breeze with a harvest moon.

Neighbours sauntering by
And often stopping to say "Hi".
Some speaking in colloquials
Others barking pastoral jovial's.

Sipping a lemonade
While watching the light fade
The stars will be out soon
Blinking to a harvest medley with the moon!

> Like a song writer
> He'd written many poems
> Favoured but a few.

The grass is green and the sky is blue
Could one imagine different hues?
Or is it just the universe in our heads?
Could a change in our brain cells paint
them with purples or reds?
And if that which we see depends
on our consciousness
Would It make difference if we were
"Conscious-less"?

I tried to imitate the mockingbird
But deception is its metier.
The harder I tried the more it laughed
In many different phrases.
Then with a wing's flash, it flew away
Chortling "queedle-ee-dee"
As if it were a blue jay.

I wish I were a weeping second hand
That could make time stand still
Whenever I feasted on happiness
Or witnessed profound goodwill.
For those precious moments vanish
in a wing's flash
And are as rare as a flighty cuckoo's
moustache.

>Aerial jewels
>Clapping wings behind their backs
>Ascend on whirlwinds.

>Watching the sunset
>An old man with distant eyes
>Transcended his age.

Praise be to all who wait
For feasts of joy or a soul mate.
Praise be to all who act
On nature's instincts or in matters abstract.
Neither patience nor action should be
disregarded
For they are not destined for the
fainthearted.

In the lull of a Zodiac spring breeze
Gently cleansed by a warm
southern mist
I rest beneath lemon-lime maples
On tender grass
Full of exciting hope
And a rainbow of mystery.

    Migrants on the beach
    Starring at the rolling waves
    Searching for lost hope.

I Hung an old bird feeder
in a nearby tree.
I filled it with peanuts
for all the birds to see.
Then I patiently waited
and waited more
But not a single bird came to explore.
Then, finally, there arrived a spritely
chickadee
Who spent the day eating merrily.
Later, as if by "word of mouth",
Others came from the N_W_E and S
More chickadees and nuthatches
and woodpeckers too.
So to my first feeder, I added number two.
The feed all gone, I was off to the store.
Then came feeders three and four.
And when the neighbour stood staring
with a frown,
I simply said, "'Tis the best theatre in town".

Fragrant blooms floating in the air
Whites as light as they dare.
Tiny pollinators spice the silence of the night
Humming quietly in the moonlight,
While exotic tall grasses and stately trees
Sway gently in the nocturnal breeze.
Not surprising that hurt-hearts unburden
While sitting peacefully in a moonlit garden.

Have you ever wondered why
Starlings murmurate in the sky?
Is it just an advancing predator they flee
That creates such synchronistic poetry?
And changing speed and direction?
Is there a telegraph somewhere in this
connection?
Scientists cannot explain the strong
correlation.
But, I did receive the communication.

She was created by the god raven
To be man's trusted companion.
She was modeled of earth
With water-grass hair -
And a life together they were to
share.

A day out of season
May seem to defy reason.
Yet, these days are increasing
As we are over-heating.
Nature appears to be out-of-sorts
The weatherman repeatedly extorts.
Perhaps it is seasonable to look afar
And hope that life will be better
On the "Red Star".

Blown off course
By the winds of his libido
And the swells of his inflated ego.
Of the price he had to pay
Little did he ever say.
And all for a brief moment of bliss
While lost in a lane lover's unholy
kiss.

Yew shapes crisp and clean
Frosts unbutton autumn leaves
To snow's enchantment.

"Other Directors"
Are always ready to direct
your play
The gates from their own
Not enough to pay their
way.

"Salt and Pepper" - "Toujours Ensemble!"
'Twas a French chef's idea of a
condomintal combo.
An edible rock and a popular spice
To be sprinkled on viandes or on rice.
For centuries a sought after cullinary team,
Hopefully, we'll see neither in our dreams.

     To those of us who have lost
     and found
     Be it a three-syllable word
     or a wandering hound
     I offer this bit of advice:
     "We must all pay the price"!
     We too must be lost before
     we are found
     'Tis nature's way with no
     way 'round.

Wool of many colours
Intertwined to explore shades
For his masterpiece.

If you have ever found your destination
With the help of a star of a constellation,
If you have ever seen your shadow in the night
In the glow of a full-moon's light
And if you have ever felt the sun
On berries picked by a loved-one
Or on a freshly harvested peach,
Then you know the heavens are not always
beyond our reach.

This light does not give colours due
But one which fades as old colours do.
The dancers once vibrant did excite
Now dull are moved out of sight.

A single kiss blown to a
lonely crow,
Elegantly,
As Glam Cherie
Don't you know?

Its shade is gone
No more to hide
Behind its scared trunk
When demons knock on the front door
In search of treasures sunk.

On the mystery of life
Questions abound.
Where did we come from?
What are we?
Where are we going?
Will there ever be explanations
Worthy of these metaphysical
questions?
Or will we have to wait
To attend at heaven's gate?

A secret admirer appeared to her
just before she passed.
Someone from her distant past.
In a clown's costume she said he
was clad
We all believed it was her fun-loving
dad.
And when her final blue gaze was
cast,
She knew she would join her
harlequin family at last.

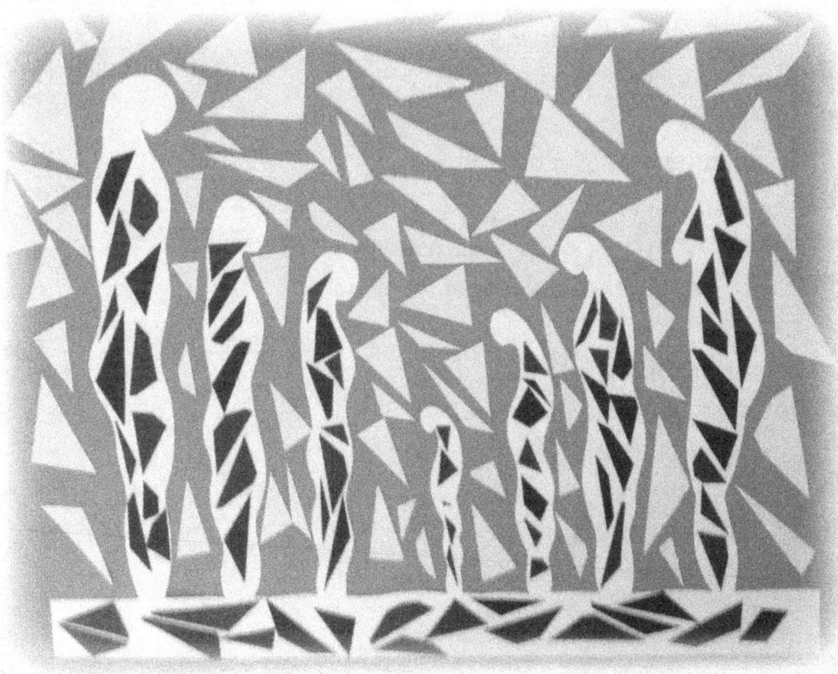

Roma was as summer sun to the rose
Giving to all life and repose.
Never a gesture to offend,
Be it family member or distant friend.
Always the last one to speak,
I can still feel autumn on her cheek.
With a heart full of grace,
She is impossible to replace.

Fallling snow on fallen leaves
Whisper requiem prayers.

There are moments of profound
inspiration
Obviously, from a superior imagination
And there are insightful works of literary
creation
Some of which have met with honest
and modest appreciation.
But, there is always the fear -
"Will the verses last over time?"
And "Was it a waste of time?"

So fragile and fair
Some with little hair
And some wrinkled and beaming
Others sedated and daydreaming
Some seemed so tired and tender
And others as if trying to remember
But all in a anticipation waiting
For a lovely death masquerading.

The rare vasc was molded with
a decorative bird.
The song of the bird was never
to be heard.
The treasured vase was of
iridescent glass
And the flight of this bird was
always "first-class".

Just passed.
There eyes blind,
Their mouths agape
And their skin cooling,
They are enshrouded in sacred silence
And stillness
And peace.
But love for them endures
Beyond the horizon of their sight,
The boundaries of their breath
And the territories of their thoughts.

Devoted friends for over sixty years
When a sudden impasse appears -
An innocuous unfulfilled promise.
Could it have been so dishonest?
They never spoke a word thereafter.
Now, they both rest in the hereafter.

The light is a little dimmer.
The joy is a little glimmer.
Even now the waves of sorrow linger
Timely recalled by the mind's bell-ringer.
Will they ever ebb away?
Or are they destined here to stay?
After all, their voyage is done
And their rewards in the hereafter have
been won.

    Equine butts windward
    Like solitary statues
    They stand defiant.

    Fragmented clay pots
    So imperfect, such beauty
    To ever embrace.

Living in a mystery can be
disconcerting -
Created by whom?
Or what? - Always averting.
Is there an eternal afterlife?
Or just this brief earthly life?
Science may solve the
enigma by and by -
Or we ourselves after
breathing our last sigh.

    The old horse staggered
    It's back swayed and lips drooped
    Beauty lay within.

    In the potting shed
    Restoring broken clay pots
    And parts of one's self.

Celestial pearls in a downward flight
Onto the tin roof like starlings light
The horses within "spook" with fright
Which by their nature is their right.
The riders from their saddles bale
And through the air to ground they sail
Tumbling with taut reins still in hand
To gain control with soft command.
The terror dissipates as they stand
Restoring trust between horse and man.

> After a spring rain
> Smells of geosmin fill the air
> My senses rejoice.

> Weaving their silk orbs
> Symphonies in gossamer
> For the world to hear.

"Willow Little Willow"
Like the zephyr through your boughs
doth flow
On my heart your love
the breeze bestow
Blind cupid's errant arrow
Dispatched from his fateful bow
so many years ago.
That I knew then
what I know now -
Courageous Lau Siu Lau.

Falling in love can be a painful
distraction
But, 'tis so hard to deny this mysterious
attraction.
What is it in you that I so adore?
Yet, would that I had many hearts to
love you more.

It was a fastball
Swinging hard it was fouled off
Batter smelled the burn.

The poet's words evaporated in
the heat of the sun
For his inspiration focused now on having
fun
The beach, the concerts, the parades on
King
With hotdogs and ice cream and beer
mugs to cling.
He's given respite to the metre, the couplet
and the rhyme
He's "Gone Fishin'" - after all
It's summertime.

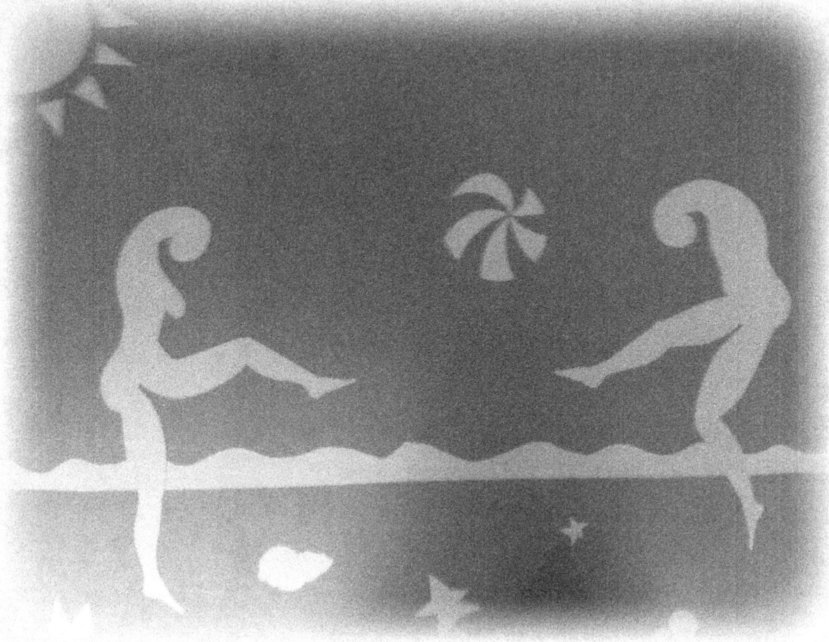

I dared to pose
metaphysical questions
to the starry sky:
From where did we come?
Why are we here?
And to where are we going?
Its answer was immediate
and yet profound:
"Just look around!"

Most things have an explanation
Except that which explains our
own creation.
Or, in the words of my curious son
"Why are we here?" And "Where
did we come from?"
"Is there a question greater
Than 'Who is our creator?'"
And "Why am I me
Instead of a flea?"
I could have been a fish in a bowl.
Does a fish have a soul?

34

Ascent to the sky
The poetic dance begins
The bent spoon is full.

Raking autumn leaves into a pile
With robust sweeps so passional
His suit of lights marching in style
Then performs a "Veronica"
exceptional.

Crossing straight lines on grass
While meticulously circling the trees
Then executing the "natural" pass
As the excited crowd waves white
hankies.

Spiralling through branches and golden leaves
Leg lifted like a cannon giving flight
While my mind delivers recitatives
The street lights appear to brighten the night.

Shortest at midday
And longest at dawn and dusk
My dark side follows.

The brilliant defence counsel pleaded with
flair
But, the truth was somewhere up in the air
Between what the defendant declared had
been
And what the confused witnessed alleged
he'd seen.
Finally, the judge had had enough
And questioned the witness to call his bluff
Like a deck of cards he folded
Then by the angry judge was scolded.
The ruling was in favour of the defendant
And the plaintiff became the offendant.
The moral: "Be careful when you sue!"
Because often the loser could be you.

In the after-storm,
Skipping stones between the waves
To the song of birds.

Sun kissed face of day
Driving his chariot west
Helios fire burns.

Holding her delicate hand
As if she were the child of Mary
Magdelland,
Her Nono cast a noble stare
Then softened his expression with a
prayer:
"Above all, I have so loved thee
But now you must let me be."
Then, with a gentle squeeze,
he turned his lolling head
And moments later he was dead.

A seashell to transport the ocean
And pride in our devotion,
As hard to understand
As a lily stuck in sand.

Beauty would be lost
If the rose had bloomed longer
Like that of a stone.

Hidden in cedar
As a farmer herded sheep,
Thrushes sang their song.

Adorned in purple
Princess trees wave in the wild
Without a country.
"Arbor non grata."

In love, we are one another
And our dreams are of each other.
Was there acquiescence from above
That we should be so in love?

I was so young and Luba was so old
But just how old, I was never told.
Her breath a wordsmith might describe
Despite copious nips of apple cider
she'd imbibe.
She gently licked salty tears when I wept
And cuddled warmly beside me when I slept.
We were best of friends or so I thought
Like King Arthur and Cavall in Camalot.
But her canine heart belonged to another-
A old stray mongrel and a frequent lover.
They were last seen walking in the morning cold
Just what happened to them, I was never told.

Every leaf is different
As is every grain of sand
Nature is so magnificent
To give "identity" a helping hand.

High liner sits deep
Haddock swim among the cod
Predators do cull.

The sun in winter
Like a distant galaxy
Had little to say.

Between grief and joy the battle persists
And wages upon my mind
For whenever the latter exists
The former is never far behind.

How can it be that I love her so
But she not me?
Is there no equity in love
To ensure reciprocity?
I am in tears with a broken heart
Being slowly torn apart.
Must I endure this painful situation
With no hope of compensation?
Is there no mechanism for redress
Each day, I become more depressed?
Heaven help me! I cannot carry on.
Surely, there is a wise, old Cupid
I can impose on.
But alas, the arrow missed its mark
Now, I wander desperate in the dark.

When will it be
That I will know what will be?
Must I wait for eternity
Before this mystery is explained to me?

The northwest wind blows
And wet snow rolls.
Metaphors and abstractions abound
And painful memories confound.
T'is a season, we dare not know
Where snow falls on snow on snow.

Holding hands to sleep
Rafting slowly down river
Tired otters dream.

Spring training is here
"Dust devils" run the bases
On their way to Mars.

The neighbourhood hawk
Swoops among stands of white pines
Screaming kee-eeee-arr.

I sing to the birds
And often they answer me
So like a duet
Vibrato not mine!

At dusk appears the firefly
In synchronistic luminescence.
Nature's pyrotechnic display in July
FIlled with the hope of romance.

When perched or in flight
The sweet songs of meadowlarks
Bring joy to our lives.
And they are fleeting
Moments of such happiness
'Til "the feast" moves on.

Tween sleep and wakeness
Paralyzed indecision
And too weak to move.

Pepita had no flowers with which to adorn
And placed weeds on the altar instead.
From thence the Star of Bethlehem was born
And painted in brilliant crimson red.

I awake in a mystery created by a mystery
Just having dreamt of this mystery
I'm now to participate in this mystery
To sustain this mystery
And advance to a state enshrouded in mystery
For the sake of a mystery
Should I choose to believe in this mystery.

> I look into your sad eyes
> As we say our goodbyes.
> Our tender kiss
> Fills me with bliss.
> As loving as can be,
> I feel like "crying happy"!

In my solitude, on a day one summer,
While grieving my beloved mother,
A "catbird" struck the window
Where I sat just below.
It then flew off like a dart
Leaving a drop of blood in the shape of a heart.
Was this a mother's message
Delivered by the bird's unfortunate passage?
And was it meant to comfort me
For of mothers, she was "a per se"!

The priest sang "Let your faith be stayed!
All your fears and doubts will be allayed!
Be not troubled by what the future may bring
God is the creator of everything!"
But what if this message is wrong?
Could there be a different song?
Or should we be rational
And accept "the wager" as did Pascal.

My color-spattered words
Like abstract expressions of freedom
Fell silent on the gallery floor.
Should I have written more?
Should I have stopped long before?
Should I have bent my words like notes
As in one of Myles' famous quotes?
Who can truly understand
If one is not a player in the band?

Ever in search of elusive love
Like a butterfly the milkweed blossom
I ride the wind high above
On a seasonal journey never forgotten.

    Hickory fall winds
    Bid the hummingbirds goodbye
    In fading ambers.

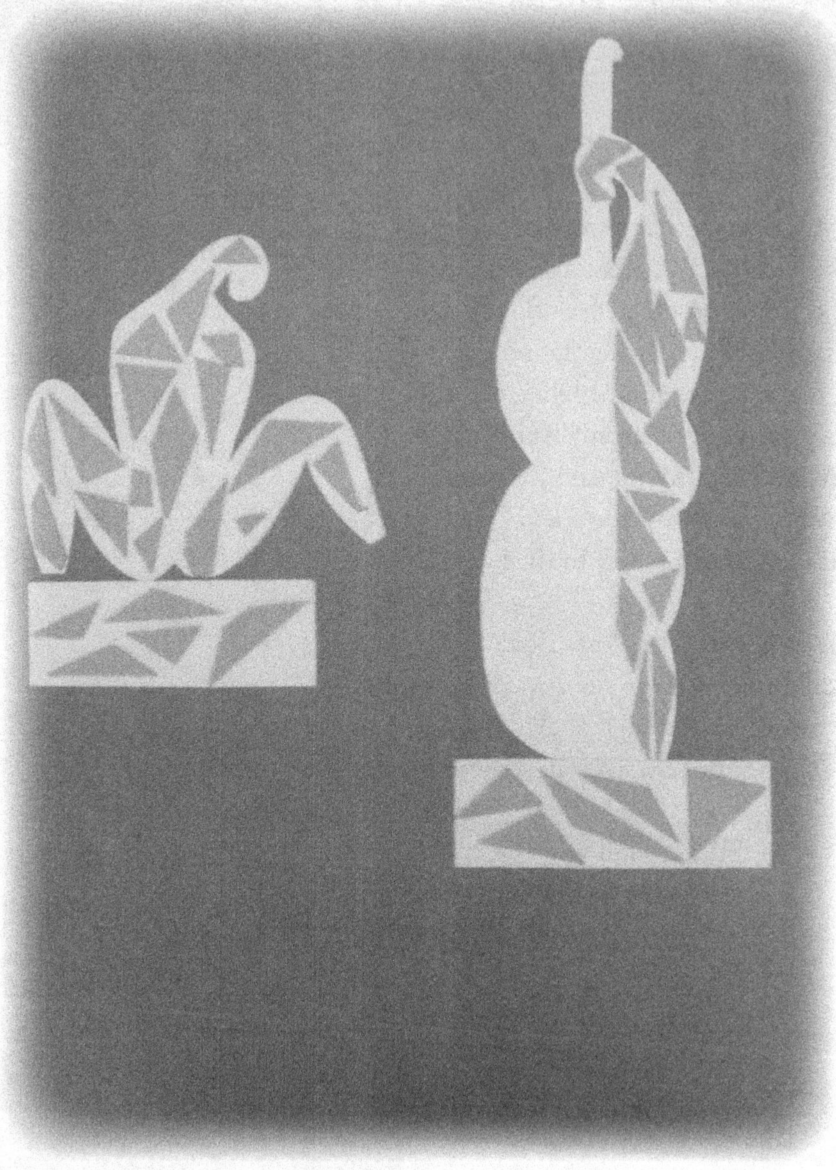

The nor' easter blew across the surging sea
Churning swells of aqua fury
The sharks attacked midst breaking waves
As shackled slaves sank into their graves.
Sun swirls and clouds of grey
Overcast the horrors of that day
And as the ocean heaved with streaks of blood,
Raging thunder spoke for a disapproving God.

The reds and greens are gone at last
Where heartaches reemerge from the past
And loneliness, the minds bell ringer,
And sadness in the voice of a carol singer.

What is more elite?
A poem or a painting?
The pen or the brush?

Bastards "golden age"
And who could have foreseen it?
"The Renaissance Man".

A paradigm of eccentricity
He excited all when he played
A genius In technique and tonality
Whose life was anything but stayed.
A man so disconsolate
He often performed through pain
Once paid with butter and chocolate
He was known to the man in the lane.
An icon of his art
And a legend though tragic
He played from his broken heart
And was called "the last romantic".

Some view the world as an end
While others a means to an end
Pleasure and freedom
Or the attainment of God's kingdom
Cupiditas and *Caritas*.
The conflict persists, as it always has.

Smooth sand pebbles dance
As strings of waves ebb and flow
And castanets clack.

The jar emptied as they fed
And sprinkled shells on the snow
In the morning and at dusk
As the winter wind did blow.
Then at night the others came
To gather round the pole
Searching for the leavings
But there was very little whole.

In what dimension am I thinking
Is it a stone that I am flinging
Or is it an event I cannot see
Destined for another reality.

Time feels so real
But does it exist?
Or is it just countless events
Designed to make sense of our
existence.
Are we a planet of innocence
And time just ignorance?

Will my love for thee
Outlive the life of me?
Will your love for me
Outlive the life of thee?
When will it be
That I will know what will be?
Must I wait for eternity
Before this mystery is
explained to me?

If I am not myself when I sleep
"How can I sin?"
If there is not commission
"Is there consent?"
They are not actions but happenings
Happenings without choices.
"How can we commit misdeeds in
our dreams?"
And if we did consent
"Are we responsible for this
'languor'? this 'visco'?"
If the answer is "No!"
"Why did he confess to them?"

Baba can you tell me
"What are we?"
Baba can you tell me
"Where did we come from?"
Baba can you tell me
"What does my future hold?"
Baba "How do you know?"

As eve turned to day
A star shone bright
Guiding us along our searching way
Through the darkness of midnight
To a place we were destined to be
For one we were destined to see.

The rains came early
Like "sin eaters" at a wake
Cleansed the plagued landscape.

Frozen in winter
And born again in spring
Iced in darkness but still alive
How is it possible to survive?
A meraculous revival
Known to some as the "frogcycle".

The whispering voices of the willow trees
Sing mournful requiem melodies
In membrance of gardens buried in snow
As the north wind adjusts its endless blow.
The maples feeding sap sit bare
And the perched raven stands a stare
While the white pines with passion sing
Of their miraculous resurrection in the spring.

Chants to deer drum beats
Midst smoke of burning sweet grass
And kinnikinnick.

A flock of starlings above the river fly
Turning and twisting dark shadows in the sky.
What can explain their mysterious show
Hypnotizing raptors as they go?

    The night turned to day
    And the stars and moon faded away
    At last to be re-born
    Into a new and real morn
    As bad dreams in sleep enthralled
    Could no longer be recalled.

    I stumbled through a thick fog
    And thought I saw the black dog
    On a hill a climb too steep
    Then at once I began to weep
    For no other reason
    Then the gray day and the season.

Raking autumn leaves in clover,
As "qana" falls like a mourning cloak,
And my black dog, "Homer"
Searches for truffles beneath the oak.
There's the last race on the river
Sails "wing on wing"
Thoughts of old age "never!"
Only hopes of an early spring.

> Waiting in the blind
> A hard freeze on the river
> The timing was right.

> Hunters wait the shot
> Ducks cup their wings and curled
> back
> Sun fades at their backs.

The solution I could not resolve
There must be some mistake
For to this level I did not evolve
Until I was awake.
I tried so hard to scream
It must have been a dark dream.

The crimson star sat in the hall
It's dried leaves beginning to fall
The ornaments of red and green
Once cherished could no longer be seen
A cheer beginning to reappear
Must be the time of year.

My head spinning like a dreidel
I lay unconscious in "the cradle"
Overwhelmed by sublime beauty
I fainted in aesthetic ecstasy.
The last moment I recall
Was David standing
contrapposto in the hall.

A pareidolia face from his past
Coalesced but did not last
Dispersed by the afternoon breeze
It disappeared among the trees
Now left with a memory to reforget
Of a youth filled with regret.

This vision so confounds
The "Spring Carol" playing
Sung by a choir of clowns
In the month of maying.
I tried so hard to sing
'Twas a "spring dream of
spring".

Hawks circled rainbows
To beats of primitive drums
And ancient sun chants.

"Sorry John Gunn!"
For snowballs thrown at you on the run
And always playing "nicky nicky nine doors" -
"On yours!"
For stealing your mullberries
("The idea for that was Harry's!")
And soaping your windows on hallowe'en -
"How cruel I must have been!"
And most of all for not trying to be your friend
Because you were alone and near life's end.
"Sorry John!
Even though you're dead and gone
I guess I was just too young!

> The wheel of fortune spins on high
> And as the betting symbols pass by
> I place "a wager" on "the Lord" -
> To cover my options before I die.

In the afterglow
The hummingbird sits its branch
On guard through the night.

Bird in the tree top
Sings its mating melody
As an act of faith.

Warm summer raindrops
Slide down leaves of gerbera
Like crystalline tears.

Swirling in rainbows
In a dance to the drum's beat
With ancient splendour.

Dense white smoke from the chimneys swirl
And the green leaves of the rhodas curl
If winter weather we are to know,
When looking out the kitchen window.

...then came the plaques and the tangles
And my life now in shambles.
The constant wondering...
And direction pondering...
The memory loss...
And a head full of rose moss.
Why the anger?
I cannot answer.
So too, the frustration
And lack of motivation.
Will I ever be the same?
By the way, "What is your name?"
I fear my own oblivion
And being unaware of everyone.
Will they remember me
And the way I used to be
Or not...
Pater Noster!...Pater Noster!...

In scholarly pursuits of my youth
I often pondered:
"Is it only by reasoning that we know
what is and is not the truth?
"Or is there a part for intuition
In making an informed decision?"
"And instincts developed long ago?"

'Tis a drug like no other
This passionate love for another
So profoundly rare and tender
A love that lasts forever
While loving is a common occurrence
The truest happens only once.

> The sun fades out of sight
> Without a prayer to mark
> the end of day
> I bow my head and instead
> Greet the onset of the night.

The sugar dance in stall await
A flat-handed treat so sweet
Performing a haute ecole gate-
Alternating diagonals of freshly
polished feet.

Freezing rain on frozen ground
And new ideas on closed minds
While angry rivers run full crown'd
Man's intolerance blinds.

In sleep, death we court.
C'est la petite mort!

While I slept
In death crept.
In a sense
'Twas non-existence.
Then in the morn
I was reborn.
But in between
There was nothing to glean.

Dazed and desolate
Unaware of the why's
A life blessed with enviable fate
Now stung by wingless butterflies
With only moments to wait
And forever close her eyes.

Morning dew on the dried petals of a rose
Sipped by a migrating butterfly
Which kissed the queen on the thigh
Why she had to die no one knows.

The crimson star stands fading in the hall
It's dried leaves like snow feathers fall
The ornaments of red and green
Once cherished are no longer seen
Comfort and cheer reappear
And blues fade with the joy of the new year.

With millions of like planets in our galaxy
How do we now define reality?
And think in what demension
To understand our creation?
Was it the "Big Bang" theory?
And will we experience the "Big Crunch"
theory?

Is there a primary cause
Or did this all happen "just because"?
And was there anything
Before the "Big Bang"?
Or was "beginningless-ness" the
explanation
For our mysterious creation?

> He was sent from God
> A legend like no other
> Leaving "love, love, love!"

If love is a neurosis,
Is there a cure?
And if there is a misdiagnosis,
How much pain should one endure?

And does love begin in October-
at noon?
And end in December-
at midnight?

And when does love
become obsession?
Is there a definite time
of inception?

Or is it all mere speculation?

The Augusta doll sits on the mantle
Dimly lit by a flickering candle.
An historic fool to be taken lightly
But, so essential to the human psyche.

I rise to greet morn
A mystery to be solved
One last day could not.

Drip, drip, drip!
Like morning dew from
blades of grass
Then like a silent stream into
death did pass
Slip, slip, slip!

A red rose was wilting "in extremis"
When a butterfly fluttered with a kiss
Like a silk angel perched on a
deathbed
And soon the rose was lovely dead.

Passionate screams of shocking disbelief
Bent with heartbreak and numb with grief,
An old life reached a determined
conclusion.
What was the reason for this preemptive
decision?
Was it made with undue force
Precluding nature from taking its course?

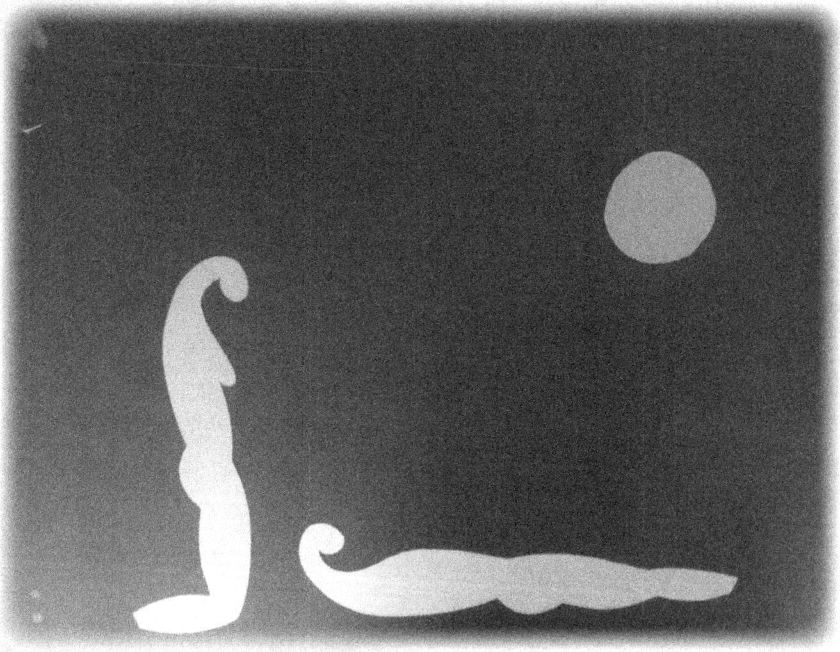

When you joyfully danced 'round that puddle
My instincts alerted me to trouble
As my heart became arhythmic
Watching you with your smile so beatific.

My emotions ran unchecked
Yours was a scene Renoiresque
And I became enchanted in the drizzle
When I heard your girlish giggle.

Nocturnal migrants silently in flight
Heard overhead but out of sight
Whether guided by magnetic fields or a star
They always know where they are.
And when I find myself afar
I follow my heart to where you are.
Homeing back to the same tree
No matter how far the distance be.

Melodious hymns of destiny and fate
Of tragic passage from here to eternity
Sung like angels at heaven's gate
As though all transgression had been
hyperbole
And as if a butterfly on the wing in migration
Assured a utopian destination.

    A broken clay pot
    A sweet metaphor for life
    Birth of something new.

I wish I knew a friendly seer
To whisper sage advice in my ear,
And dedicate some magical feat
While never yielding to deceit
And willing always to prophesize
While hiding behind a unique disguise.

There is "a calm" beneath that old
"grandfather" tree
As if it had seen all there was to see
And was at peace with its own destiny
After witnessing generations of
children's glee
Especially in the autumn when
chestnuts fall
As it shares its bounty among them all.

With millions of like planets in
our galaxy,
How might Angelicus now
explain their creation?
Would he still opine "ex nihilo"
Or proffer a different revelation?
And might he not be leery
Of the rational behind the "Big
Bang" theory?

> The "Apricots" were picked
> Then the trees were uprooted
> The "Grove" was flipped
> And no longer fruited.
> Houses in the old orchard -
> who's to blame?
> Even though they kept
> its original name.

An admiralty anchor was propped up on his
lawn
Brownie's young face was pale and draw
Lying with his "teddy" beside him in bed
A few days later, he was dead.
The anchor now rusted still rests in place
Never will I forget my young friend's face.

> "I lived here before!"
> My memory can't recall
> And I couldn't have.

A soulful stare
A mother's desperate prayer
The last words spoken
As tender hearts lay broken.
Another life has reached an early
conclusion
Or, is it just a mysterious illusion?
And after this life from which he
departed,
Will he go back to where he started?

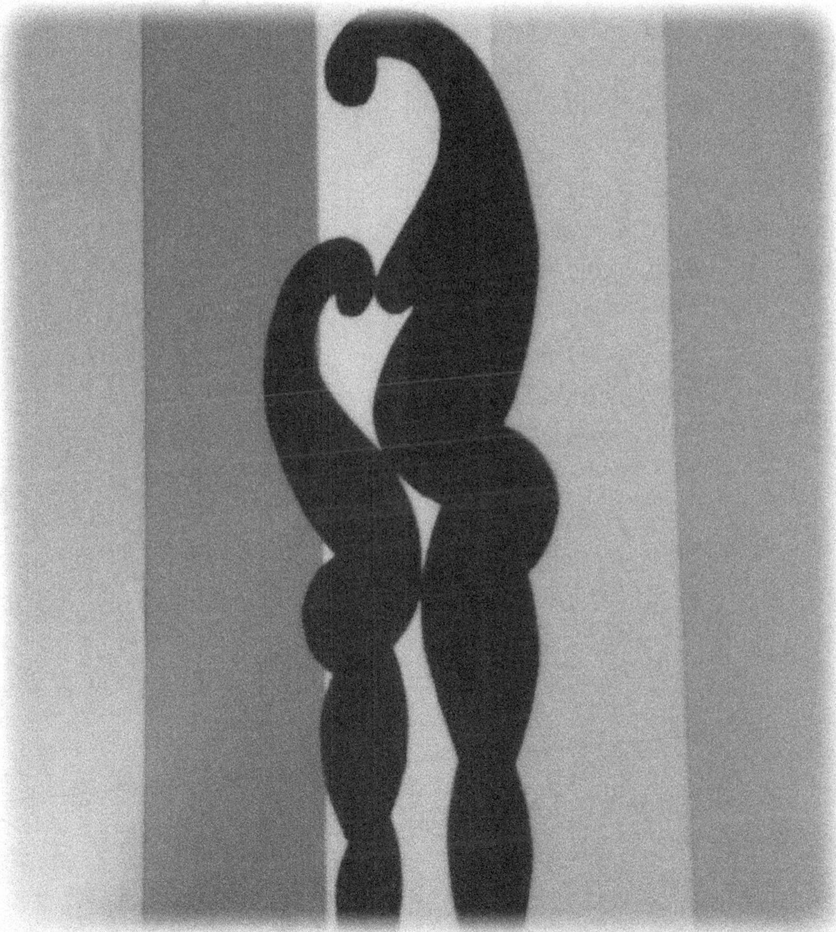

The cries of a child
Awakened instincts in me
I want to know "why?"

Alas, how can it be?
I loved her so much and she not me.
What was it in her I did not see?
Was it just a lovers' mystery?
Surely, it had nothing to do with me
When she pleaded she wanted to be free.

The breeze in the woods
Flipped coloured leaves in the air
To carpet the ground.

Pebbles surfed the beach
As sky blue eyes blinked calmly
Constant was the wind.

As a force of natural selection
Your beauty is a matter of evolution
Causing a rush of "Darwinian" suitors
And attracting unwanted predators.

I am bruised and beset by competing rivals
Performing challenging recitals.
Is there nothing we can do
To prove to all our love is true?

    Freedom and reason
    While often antinomous
    Seem always in season
    Though occasionally amorphous.

    Tundra swan wedges
    Herding up the grand river
    Fly in ground effect.

Born to seek power
And not to cower
A similar behaviour of "man" and "ape"
A common evolutionary root there's no escape.
As in Machiavelli's "Prince" or Rheinhold's
"Affe einen Schadel betrochtend"
If we could only accommodate them
It would settle scores of old.

    The embryonic universe
    Where nothing was yet named
    As particles throughout space disburse
    And in each of us contained.

    From one point of energy and matter
    The universe was created
    Laying foundations for the answer
    To the greatest question ever debated.

And then came the "Big Bang"
Before which nothing had a name
And all is speculation
From point of energy to universe
expansion.
The body of it is in us contained
Though not often wisely explained:
"Your memories
are my memories!
And my universe
is your universe!"

There was a conflict last night
Between my ego and my soul
My ego wanted to fight
The other wanted to console.
Free from the constraints of the ego
To pursue a higher goal
My soul now with one it hardly knew-
Its devine guru.

Running before the wind
With square sails set
The Calimas advance oil laden
Minoan ships
Destined for the Garden of the
Hesperides,
The three nymphs of evening
and the golden light of sunsets.

A rare force felt but not understood
So like communication with God.
Out of heartbreak and despair
So often a curse without care
Flow the arts that transcend
From a mysterious source
known as "duende".

In the wolf moonlight
Shadows kiss on sparkling snow
I hear a lone howl.

Chalk and brushes flying through the air
The frazzled young teacher trying to resume
Though none of the students seemed to care
"It is the east, and Juliet is the sun!"
Falling on deaf ears all but one
Whose love of Shakespeare had just begun.

Gone is the sun
Just as a daystar that has flickered away
And like the sun
My love has gone away.
Now in darkness I'm alone
My romance no longer where you are
Dreaming of a universe unknown
Since my heart is now a dead star.

Were I to sow a nocturnal kiss
Would I reap your diurnal love?
Or would you condemn me to the liss
As I cursed the "blinking" stars above?

"Half for you and half for me!"
'Tis nature's way and must always be.
Observe the golden honeybee
Resting on a red stripe for three
On a flag of an island in the sea
To realize our own destiny.

How old am I?
About 15,000 years or so
And I am not yet ready to die!
It is time to pass the "talking stick"
As I have spoken!

When the mystery in which we live
Outlasts the world in which we live
Will it all have been forgot
Will all creations and endeavours have been
for naught?
What will remain of what we know-
The sky above and the earth below?
And will love morph into yet another sphere
Where the mystery is solved and extinction
does not appear?

I live in a glass house
With no walls and no rooms.

There are lively reflections on the glass
As people from all walks pass.

In but out ...
Out but in...

Ever-changing through weather and season
I see the sunset and the moon rise
At the same time, standing in the same place.

Often, passerbys scrutinize my space
As a kaleidoscope or to glimpse my hidden face.

"Anna abola
Ess ess iola!"
(Banana split)

"Purple and yellow"
Was the colour of the frog
It wasn't my 'magination
I swear to God.

I was wading in "Tear of the Clouds"
It was raining "cats..." too
I just stuck my hand in and picked 'er up
First, I thought it was yellow and blue.

I was so bedazzled
She musta jumped from my hand
Back into where I got 'er
'Mazin' how fast I lost 'er.

My best friend and I fought one night
A heated "scrap" under a dim street light.
Many punches were thrown and it wasn't a game
Although a draw, our friendship was never the
same.

Harems hunker down
On high ground with trees and tails
To ride out the storm.

    Pests at bird-feeders
    Uninvited visitors
    The bragging should stop.

Diurnal migrant to my love must bring
A melodious message this early spring
And to your own voice you must be true
So that others will not imitate you
A love song of devotion in display flight
At break of day rising or early night
To weld our lonely hearts as one
Flying joyfully into the eternal sun.
And if in all this you will succeed
Your mission will honour love's deed.

Of many, have I written verses
But will verses be written of me?
Will my verses be studied by students
Or footnoted in academic research?
Or recited in dramatic performances
By passionate lovers or others?
Or inspire young writers who need
Inspiration?
Or, have I done it all for me
With no thought of posterity?

A poet unknown
Whose verses were read by few
And inspired by one.

Love is the truest colour that I know
And the first colour of the rainbow.